MANUAL

The **New York City Youth Poet Laureate Program (YPL)** is a spoken word competition designed to energize youth voters through poetry. The YPL Program sponsors workshops for participants, ages 13-19, to hone their writing skills and teach them about voting and community leadership. After the workshops, students submit poems about voice, voting and civic engagement to a panel of judges. The judges select 12 finalists based on the applicant's poetry portfolio, performance technique, and commitment to civic engagement. These finalists then compete in a NYC Voter Poet Final Slam, where the Youth Poet Laureate is named. The winner works to promote civic engagement throughout the city during the election year. The NYC Youth Poet Laureate represents Urban Word NYC, the New York City Campaign Finance Board (CFB) and the Voter Assistance Advisory Committee (VAAC) in their outreach throughout the city to communities in need and potential youth voters.

Founded on the belief that teenagers can and must speak for themselves, **Urban Word NYC™** (UW) has been at the forefront of the youth spoken word, poetry and hip-hop movements in New York City since 1999. Urban Word NYC presents literary arts education and youth development programs in the areas of creative writing, journalism, college prep, literature and hip-hop. UW provides FREE, safe and uncensored writing workshops to teens year round, and hosts the Annual NYC Teen Poetry Slam, NY Knicks Poetry Slam, Voter Slam, local and national youth slams, festivals, reading series, open mics, and more. Urban Word NYC believes that free self-expression - matured in an enhanced critical literacy environment - improves self confidence and strengthens educational achievement for NYC's inner city youth. We promote active literacy, critical thought, and positive social dialogue across boundaries of age, race, class, gender, culture, and sexuality. Our many workshops are designed to enhance critical thinking skills, leadership, and to ignite a personal commitment to growth and learning which leads to heightened in-school performance, and greater interest in pursuing higher education.

The **Campaign Finance Board** promotes voter registration, voting, and civic engagement through community outreach and partnerships with public and private organizations. Under the banner **NYC Votes!** and with the assistance of the Voter Assistance Advisory Committee (VAAC), the CFB coordinates voter events, distributes voter education materials, and helps NYC residents register to vote. In 2009, the CFB partnered with Urban Word NYC to develop a youth voter education campaign that would increase voter participation and awareness amongst youth voters. Now in its third year of the program, the Youth Poet Laureate program has successfully registered new youth voters, and during the month of April alone, the program was able to take the message of the importance of voting to over 5,000 NYC students. This year's program has expanded exponentially to include tours of NYC Libraries, High schools, and Parks. The Rockefeller Foundation was a key supporter of this innovative program, along with the help of recent partnerships which include: WNBC, NYC TV, NYCHA, U.S. Census, NY Historical Society, NYC Board of Elections, the City University of New York, and Hot97.

MANUAL

JUSTING LONG-MOTON

Penmanship Books
Brooklyn, NY

Penmanship Books
Published by Penmanship Publishing Group

593 Vanderbilt Avenue, #265
Brooklyn, NY 11238

Copyright © 2011 Justin Long-Moton
Cover Design by Rico Frederick

All rights reserved. This book may not be reproduced in whole or in part (except in the case of reviews) without written permission from author.

First Penmanship trade edition: November 2011
To contact **Justin Long-Moton** please visit www.penmanshipbooks.com.
ISBN# 978-0-9831219-5-4
Printed in The United States of America
10 9 8 7 6 5 4 3 2 1

for you, and what it took to get you here

TABLE OF CONTENTS

Manual	9
STEP 1	11
Blueprint's Blues	13
In the beginning	14
Dick & Jane	15
First Dates	16
12D	17
Inkblots	18
Dodging Traffic	19
The Mechanic	20
STEP 2	
Who Broke You?	23
Lynch Kentucky	24
Sharpshooter	26
Salvation's Cauldron	28
The Shop	30
You're a Dead Man Walking	32
Confessions of a Suicide Note	33
Can I Live Here?	36
STEP 3	
Second Dates	38
Hinges	39
Shattering Water	41
Monsoon Season	42
Speaking to Flames	43
Missing Page: THE KIDS	44
Bloodlines Lament	45
Con Artist AKA	46
Dog Breeders	47
The Mechanic	48

STEP 4
You Became Ice Sickles	51
Lincoln Town Car Travels	53
Ode to Ohio	55
Tree Hugger	57
0,7,1,9,9,3	58
Brew	60
Wombs Bloom	61
Carnival	62
11E	64
Sometimes all it takes is FAITH	65

WARRANTY
Philomath Says No to a Book	69
Metronome	70
Growing Down	71
Advice for when you have had enough	73
The Mechanic	74
Storks Carry Toolboxes	75
A Few Thoughts of Gratitude	78

Manual

Curtains peel back in layers
Windows clothed in misty fog
Await a finger to stitch some prophetic
Name (yours) in its wet jacket of moisture
Patches of clarity, reveal all that's beyond
This dialect of brick

It is 2:33PM
Sharp bend of road leading to common
Cobblestone driveway
Navigated by the punctual mail man
Truck comes to a gradual halt, engine idling
Synced to the day's cackling static

It is finally here
You are finally here

Mangled parcel in hands
Lend the mail man the signature
You've borrowed, you'll have your own
Soon enough
Neglect all urges to shake
Razorblade to packing tape
Its limbs will uncurl

It is not gravities steady dementia but your
Sadness causing your chin to sag
Initial disappointment is standard
Be assured, Yes, that is (this is) you
Mirage of shattered things
A life that has yet to be welded together

Instruction manual
Wedged between two pieces of Styrofoam
Printed on recycled scripture

Assembly may be difficult, but you are only
A few tightened screws away
From perfection
Everything you need is [inside]

STEP 1

ARCHITECTURE

Blueprint's Blues

Pride reddens embers. The chest's swelling signifies
I built this life from the toe up to the very hair follicles
that will surrender to time. What our hands have
potential to make of us burns casually in our mechanical
nuances. There is a constant struggle to become self.
We, the sands assembly line are collages of mishaps,
wrong turns and fates loose threads, made to believe
whole, though our sense of *incompleteness*.

In the beginning

there was me. Face chiseled marble and an earthen
screech that peeled paint from walls. My arrival
mysterious as the Big Bang was sudden. An unexpected
surge of gust, cracking windows into runways of light
and we flew in. Skies cargo, a nine month delivery made
right on schedule. Touched down on the most miserable
day of the week—Monday, hates its reflection. It is the
1st work day, rush hour traffic, a migraine lingering from
Friday night's cocktails and shimmy. A stoic July
rendered me intrusive. Held in the burrows of my
mother's arms, I imagine her gazing down in reverie,
eyes wide in awe that this life had blossomed inside her,
believing her body was unworthy of such miracles. This is
all speculation, the mind's theory on origin. Another
un-photographed genesis—no one wanted memories.
When envisioning my first breath I see: pale infant
citizen to two realms, this one and the ghostly, he is
crying with a wrench clutched in his fist.

Dick & Jane

Father is stethoscope, khaki slacks and golf on Saturday mornings.
Mother is oven mitts and cherry pie.
Bagged lunch, antique radio, shines face into kitchen floor,
Chicken casserole for the new neighbors.

Best house "on the block," eggshell white with teal trimmings, red
Brick chimney juts from top like a hand blocking sun at high noon.
Porch sturdy, smooth as the word *forgiveness*.
Fence (color already known) keeps trespassers out and dog in.

Behind wooden barricade: the lawn greedy in its green, thriving
Off good water. Blades of grass lush and thick, bloated from
The American Dream.

First Dates

She was never brimstone curled in fetal
position, he neither Romeo singing the rust off
a park swing—burnt rice and wormwood
wedding vows. My mother is miles from
submissive. Seductive maverick in her own
right, she could sweet-talk the wandering bullet
back into its barrel. My stepfather is a large
man. Bull-horn stubble, shaving the cowbells
from his chin. Steering wheel kind of faith, used
to drive buses from New York City to Out There.
I'd like to think that's how they met—she
running away from herself, and he a one-way
ticket to nowhere. A love story scribbled in
chicken-scratch cursive.
But I will be reluctant to tell my children
the truth. It will roll off the tongue in a low
whimper, like the first shovel of dirt into
a grave. I will tell them, grandma and grandpa's
eyes danced one dusty afternoon in Harlem.
He saw her slouched over, sitting on a milk
crate, with a dollar rolled into a skinny funnel.
Asked *"Do you need an extra set of nostrils to finish
that?"* She smiled.

12D

At the old apartment (new then) I'd rest on an aged fold out cot. Twirl myself into a quilted chrysalis until the potential of wings was hacked out by the unbearable heat. The cot was centered at the base of grandma's hickory closet, in there hung the coats of her past lives. I'd lie there smaller than everything breathing, except the plants, giant green creatures with leaves the size of elephant ears. They never forgot the words we didn't speak. On mornings when the scent of pancakes and bacon was snuffed out by the day priors tiring 9 to 5, the floors would pinch me from my slumber with a constant thump. I'd sit up, my body now a more contorted phrase—*You're making too much noise, I can't sleep.* She was power-walking, knees digging into chest. Grandma didn't have a six pack, but she sure looked good in her blouses (still do). Her eyes a rustic mahogany, mimicking the rocking chair the great grand's play in. Entranced by the 32inch Magnavox television we had in the living room, her blood in sync with the shifting pixels. *Sweating to the oldies*, Richard Simmons would coach her wrinkles back to juke joint and loose ankles. I'd always end up behind her, watching in admiration, with the bottom of my thighs stuck to plastic. She had our couch laminated to protect it from my spills and Grandpa Bert's jerry curl. We didn't see Bert much when he was home, stayed cooped up in his room—turtle to its shell. Watching game shows, sometimes I'd ask him why he never tried out for Jeopardy or Wheel of Fortune, he'd reply *in school my favorite subject was recess*, I'd laugh knowing he was a lot smarter than he led on to believe. Once I saw him complete three crossword puzzles in the Daily News— genius is measured in paper cuts. Every now and then he'd emerge from his lair, stagger to the fridge, grab a cold one and mosey on back. We didn't worry about Bert. The ceilings paint chipped to each new page of our story. It is bare now. The day the adoption was finalized, after the sun lent us as much light as it could, we drifted home exhausted from celebration. The lock on the front door troubling as always clicked, hinges swiveled and we were greeted by a new heir. I was 11.

Inkblots

Wednesday torso is set to recline 104°. ~~I~~ and one clean cut PhD attempt to unmask all that has yet to be claimed: past and present. Days enjoy sewing themselves to wrist and dangling like bracelet charms. Took three sessions to admit ~~I'd~~ considered strumming my veins with a paring knife to teach yesterday lessons in gravity. "What do you see in this one?" *A boy trying to outrun his footprints.* Cheeks bruise red when the lie blossoms in the mouth and not the heart. "Why must you go straight home afterschool?" *~~My~~ grandma needs me…. ~~I'm~~ going somewhere… (Stutters)* "Tell me what's going on here." *There's a boy hiding his limbs from the mirror.* Placebos trick the mind into thinking one is getting help—pills are for the insane. I didn't take them. In this room there's no need to straightjacket my tongue. Healing succeeds acceptance of self, "How about this one?" *~~Me~~ growing into my scars, ~~me~~ wounded yet smiling, ~~I~~ see ink on ~~my~~ hands, ~~I~~ see ink, and I see ink.*

Dodging Traffic

Hands interlocked with a body
well-versed in the street's diction—told
look both ways before crossing, envied
squirrel until it became our first lesson
in road kill. We ask the pavement about
dimensions, *is it possible to inflate a flat
line?* We've seen car hoods make bone
expel its marrow. To head-butt the grill
of 18 wheels is not liberation, it is faith
that someone, somewhere finds beauty
in the wreckage of you.

Red and bouncing metaphor for us,
ever shifting course of our rolling
and leaps. We are round, the chisels
offspring. It sprints into a tangle
of fog lights and hazard signs. Feet
respond faster than ribcage, get ahead
of self. Want to chase it, long for eyes
to lick asphalt and go. But, hesitation is
a seed that sprouts sporadically. Blood's
paralysis is unexpected, pot holes don't
exist until tires bleed tow truck.

Life rolls onto an empty highway—
tribulation enjoys speeding.

Fear can be uprooted. Circumstance is
not a weed to be tossed away. Dodge
what man-*made*. Rather chase dreams
and get hit, then stand at stop signs
waiting for them to turn green.

The Mechanic

Don't lie to me!, he says scolding the mirror. *I don't look
like that.* Hands outstretched, choking his reflection
until its blushing cracks, *now that's more like it*. He
believes in beauty only in its purist form—wild hedges,
sunlight, and women with no coatings. Insecurity is
the absence of applause after a cell splits. It is a lack
of praise for the perfect choreography happening
within, which makes one human. He is a chair
in an empty theater afraid to clap for his own blood.
At birth his mother let the sky name him *Wanderer*,
after wind, tide and moon. To know no bounds or
restraints is an asylum of its own and he is resident of
limitless and vagrancy. Scars remind the skin of reality.
He cannot recall a time where he felt *whole*, reason he
fills his hallows with alloys to occupy space. But, steel
bends—barrel to head will make the atheist pray. He
has relieved Atlas, place your burdens on his
fragmented shoulders. He say's *you cannot break
what's already broken, I'm okay being sacrifice.*
He is martyr. He is paste and screws for the world
and not his body. He is two eyes settled and
comfortable with everyone's happiness. He is a china
cabinet's religion after its crashing. He is a morgue for
living things. He is broke. He is fixable. He is tool, only if
heart surrenders to truth.

STEP 2

DEMOLITION

Who Broke You?

The ghetto.

Its gunshot hymnals, withered grass coated in
morning's cold syringes, mothers: nails to neck-
scratching, yesterday's caution tape, stale
Dutch wedged in back pocket, weed smoke
pollutant, liquor store within three block radius
of check cashing place, mail man's empty hands
on the 1st, a streetlight's sin in a dark alley while
a daughter takes a shortcut home, a broken
home, no hot water, palms pressed against
stove during winter's gaze, chuckle after *do you
accept food stamps*, black ankles shackled to
blacktop windmills, flower girl sprinkling
gunpowder, brother's court hearing, mail man's
empty hands on the 15th, candle light vigil
around infant's chalk outline, road trip in
hearse, the siren's echo, the sirens echo.

Lynch Kentucky

We didn't hang their ghost out long enough to dry
washboard, clothes line—its hard wringing
bones out of a spirit.

My Great Grandmother's name was Esther:
apron and fox hound, had a bite like boycott
and smiled pistol whips. She was known for her
two green thumbs and patch of land, her eyes
dilating ashtrays. Ribcage old western decor,
bar fight laughter, protests the moonshine.

Marlboro Lights and silence is all I know of my
Great Grandfather. A simple man, worked the
coal mines, called him "Big O" for Otis—godly
hands, a grip like a bear trap, he could shake
Christ out of you. He was an earthly man, never
able to crack the husk of him. Crucified
footprints, dirt roads, burning u-hauls—Klan
moved in next door.

Great Grandparents use' to bathe in onyx, bore a
last name delicate as cotton, Garner with an ER
like sirens, gurneys or an eerie house
sculpted from the pulse of one womb.

Country life—

An iron skillet playing jacks with a pot of grits,
back burner like welts, and church on Sunday
morning, in a town that tastes like nooses.
Porch swing, backyard hammock, fist full of rice,
jumped the broom—segregated blood waiting
on the other side. The air is thick with
the history of me. Here I'm white picket fence
and picket sign.

Last words—

Son, men are deserts.
Granddaddy Otis painted a barbershop
in the corner of the house, he never thought his
wife would be his only customer.

Child watch my crops, scare the Jim Crows.

Their souls begin to rise,
I take my palms to try shoving
their youth back into their bones.

They died because there were too many
crickets in their chest, crooked cops place
handcuff over a heartbeat and this is what you
call cardiac arrest.

Flat lines—

Defibrillator to the sky.
No more bullets on hotel balconies.
No fire hose baptisms.
Pink ribbons, crumbling Saint Jude,
heart shaped obituaries.
Freedom waltzes across the heavens, million
cloud march, boots laced, silver lining stride
to redemption.

I turn to the doctor and ask him,
"When will we have a cure for all this?"

Sharpshooter

You are beer bottle,
flying saucer, dart
board, something worth
piercing,
a mannequin craving
hollow tip, crimson in
the hands of cowboys,
bull's-eye, reason knife
sharpens itself, feathers
at a tea party, martyr.

You that stuck out
daffodil in a patch of
ivy, you will be target
practice. They will
launch heat seeking
slurs, meant to melt
faith and weaken any
fortress you've built
within. There will be
times you face firing
squads of eyes, and you
must convince them of
your human.

There will be riots,
pitchforks thrust up
into a charred sky.
Sidewalks will overturn,
fire will disown its
creation and attempt to
consume you. Thunder
cackles cracking
of knuckles, religion
prepares for
the fistfight.
No god, only hands,
two feet and mind
calibrated to pummel.
Teach the body
ascension and develop
juggernaut complex.
Wrap all you desire in
Kevlar.

You are a crosshair's shepherd. Lead this unholy crucifix into your fields, when they fire, duck.

Salvation's Cauldron
for Malidoma Patrice Somé

I'm years older than that moment
Meaning the clock's hands
Have awkwardly manipulated
My height, bone mass and way of thinking
Parched dry heathen of vertebrae
I still stand with a limp

Mother taught me
Morning is a flaking scab which allows
The day to bleed through
But, I bleed too that day when she left me
Alone with father
Usually he be to faith as chandeliers be to darkness
Blasphemy comes in all shapes and sizes

Remember the song our hearts jumped to
As crickets strummed their hind legs
Congregation picnic's soundtrack
I was your favorite son, you led us in grace
We ate till the sun retired to its night shed
Engrossed in feeble conversation, so malleable
Bending to my youthful intellect
I recall joyous occasions

Back then, you weren't
Splinters, scars, bruised knees,
Prosthetic grins, canines sharpened
To a thumb tack

Mother told me, at birth
She handed me to you
Stroking the small of my face, how you
Hold prayers and scriptures, delicate
Afraid that'd you'd break me like I was made of Glass
Admired the way my eyes held light
Purity in its simplest form

Tell me
Were your fangs growing then?
Webs of saliva darting through your beard
Were you a beggar's palm?
A thief's blueprint
Double shot of Jack from
A pedophile's stare

My steps—left, right
Father
You left me right?
To bathe in the heavy of you
Your scent anchor in my blood
Reason I blush purple
In the presence of a rosary

Skin stretches
But, silence can stunt your growth
I have not grown up
I'm still that boy naked
Seven calendars of aching
Choking on my beliefs
I have told no one
Shame clogs my palate
I won't be a man anymore
If someone knows of my innocence
In the collection basket
To pay your tithes and offering

Father
When do you confess?
When will the cold spit-shined
Floorboards in that church creak what they saw?
The pews have remained speechless for 19 years
Of your hands leaving sermons
Around the necks of boys who look like me
Bleached to the bone
Stain glass scratching back of throat
I'm still vomiting my faith

It has taken me nearly two decades
To confront you

I joined the choir, asked
The vocal instructor to teach me
The art of screaming

The Shop

Straight razors sharpen, scissors flutter,
afro pick, crew cut, fade.
We are the darkest of Caesars.

The shop is always open for business.
Chimes have welcomed an archive
of bodies, as sons become lambs in
the shepherding palms of their fathers
guiding them into the mouth of
manhood.

Dampened brick hole in the wall dug
into the ghastly forearm of the city's
grumpiest street. Neighborhood's
gossip coliseum, where the wise one
congregates, jazz to revolution—
Coltrane tooting Garvey.

Age bestows insight on young minded:
shave with the grain not against.

Chess and checker boards teach
young soldier's ancient war tactics.
Bootleg: e-v-e-r-y-t-h-i-n-g, DVDs, sneakers
Cologne to hide adultery's stench.

Leather chairs worn but prideful, cradle
limbs—exhaustion evident in hue.

Barbers hand steady, unwavering in its
faith as wind creeps beneath base of
the door calm, phantom silent, ready to
test the *will* of each strand laden along
marble, awaiting rapture of locks.

There is a child, restless, static
collecting in his knees, begging mother
for more than wooden nickels; he
shakes the gumball machine believing a
contusion will award him two pieces for
his 25¢.
In another corner, costumers wait patiently
for their turn under the blade.

For the son unaware of his light's origin,

the shop is an adoption agency. He
knows between the hours of 10-7 there
is a man willing to lend the raspy
baritone of him. The shop's tongue is
chameleon, blending into circumstance.
In times of discipline it is the belt's whip
lash. For he that is wet behind the ear,
virgin to love and the magnetism of in
betweens, it is romance novel sung into
silk garbs, a gentlemen's perfect suit.

Conversations linger, discussions
concerning mundane and controversial.

*Black man aint got no place in a white
man's army. It's not sanitary.*

*I use to cut young blood's hair in this
very chair, good to see he making it in
the pros, I know his momma proud.*

OJ did it, end of conversation

(Fitting) The sky once white like a pair
of alabaster gloves begins to churn
scarlet—dipped in the ghetto's oldest
blood.

You're a Dead Man Walking
for my brothers

Vibrates skull—skipping of smooth
stones across the sober face of a pond
warning, echoing through bone

Yet, the gallows can't hold this molten
black, nonchalant toward reaper's
knocking: revolver becomes signature
for negotiations with death, invalid-
barrel's smoke doesn't heave in cursive

You're a dead man walking

But, black boy (black brother) doesn't
believe in *The Man's* rope burn, cannot
handcuff this myth of flesh saddled to
charred yesteryears, riding through
the ghetto on a ration of crack rock
stallion, addictive buck distributed
evenly amongst cousins of poverty,
satisfied being: fiend's wet dream,
beauty's carcass

You're a dead man walking!
Mother warns

Becomes a turned shoulder, spit in
the face of Lady Day, old (new) western
dust

....
Vibrates skull

Like the pond, black boy
(black brother) will miss his ripples,
once the tongue grows tired of
throwing caveat stones—just to be
ignored.

Confessions of a Suicide Note

If you have found me
They're long gone by now
Bones wilting into cob webs
Waiting for their wings to be welded
To their backs
Angels must earn their feathers

*

Andrew
I should've known after the first black eye
But you convinced me this hurt was a birthmark
3 years of mascara and tinted sunglasses
A gal can only fall down a flight of stairs
But so many times before people start asking questions
I've spent the last moments of my life apologizing
For things whether they were my fault
Or not
Do not think
For one moment you are the sole
Reason I am doing this

*

Russian roulette with the medicine cabinet
Pill bottles snake charm my demons
The bathroom floor will
Hold me like those trenches
Honey, I'm still shaking the soil from my boots
Trying to find home
It's just the television's static
Reminds me of their faces
Last night, the theater manager
Asked if I was old enough to see this movie
I stared in his eyes, I saw he's never been to war
Never picked his teeth with a grenade pin
Had his palm—gauze pressed against
A screaming geyser trying to stop
Your fellow soldier from bleeding to death
I told him *I killed 18 people, and you want to see*
My identification
I can't live with this, their throbbing hearts
Burdening my breath
Baby, I got to go before they send me back
Tell them they can keep their flag

*

Dad,
This time there's really a skeleton hanging
In your closet

*

To make this easier
Let's just say the razor slipped

*

This pension check isn't doing it
Can't buy her more steps
Only oil to stop her wheelchair from crying
Under her heavy
This note is for the both of us
I can't bear to see my wife of 53 years
Rotting
While the hospitals
Collect payment for treatment
That isn't working
Hands out, callused in the art
Of carving coffins
If something is going to kill her
It might as well be me
By the time you get here, she'll be tucked in
Resting peacefully like a woman who knows
Something about pearly gates
I'll be out back, back broken knock-kneed
Split fractured wishbones
Begging whomever's in charge up there to grant
Her a new set of legs

*

I'm sorry mom
I don't think you knew
I like *he* who's best for me
But, in college they don't accept that
I'm sure the Hudson do
Been running from my lips
From the moment they stumbled upon
Another man's
I've kept my life private
You see this white boy, thin wire spectacles
What did I ever do to them momma?
I understand my skin reeks of what America hates
I'm not straight, but why couldn't my roommates

Let my spleen be crooked coat rack holding gay flesh
Hurled my business
Into the teething mouth of the internet
The cat's out of the closet
Floating down river
Don't cry mom
I'm free now
Love always, Tyler

    *

If you have found me
The ink has dried
I am but a testament to their existence
The last words of life, scrolled across skin

Can I Live Here?

Peace is a wishbone snapping
to a free verse of metal.
When heart could find none in
this dimly lit chest cavity it
sought out an alternative
dwelling place.

My notebook was never meant
to be a meat cleaver. Just
a bucket of pocket watches
I'd soak my feet in after long
hours of dreaming. Stumble
home, fatigue carving itself into
a yawn. I'd maneuver my body
into a rocking chair's maple
wood teeth and dizzy ship
anchor myself into nostalgia.
It was to be house built from
memories.

A dining room of butchered
palms left juggling knives
and forks, a family of wrists
desperately trying to slice
yesterday into smaller pieces,
easier to chew and forget.

When heart skipped out on
body it left its pulse, wanted no
remnants of oppression. Leave
the beating behind, page teach
dead things stillness
and revival.

Here in this home designed by
quills I am fist fights against
demons.

Heart found more than mattress,
found sanctuary between
margins. It worships walls that
have sworn not
to crumble.

STEP 3

DUST SETTLES

Second Dates

The serrated side of a knife will chase
a man from his home—step-father is no
exception. He is a crack house Harlem
mortgages, flame tarnishing silverware. Mother
is a plague of accusations, after late nights she'd
search his collars for the lipstick smears of ghost
(nonexistent). *I know you've been sleeping
with_____* (the babysitter).
He is snake slithering to avoid argument
and vacant side of the bed. Mother is a
nightmare's aftertaste—mixture of nicotine and
road, reason for his vanishing. My step-father is
treasure hidden within mausoleum. He is
the strongest brick, laid in the wrong building,
his frowns are stress cracks. After his departure,
mother borrowed a blank stare from the empty
street. She became the hypnotist's secretary,
numb to everything outside her pulse (even me).
When wedding bells begin to rot and spoil, not
even the salt in a child's tears can preserve love.
Together they are rose trapped in a thorn bush. I
lived amidst the rubble of their
marriage. Eventually the cops came to pry me
from the debris. To this day, I stand in the rain
because I'm still rinsing off the ash.

Hinges

5 things to consider when opening a door

    1.   Notice the noises seeping through the cracks

The radio in the next room has never been this loud.
Music can mask the unholy, I realize now there are lies
imbedded in every note. Once the brass knuckles of day
have unfolded, I'll ask that jungle fisted horizon to
punch my yesterdays back into skull—many doors
in my mind, thoughts pendulum swaying iron and wood.
Memories tormented, stuffed between the cracks.

I'm here—standing, silent as white noise.
Unsure of what's waiting on the other side, the secrets
ducking beneath the shadows. However, the unknown
tempts me. Eardrums aged 9 years, bathing
in the sound of moaning crescendos.

She told me, *stay*, dog's tongue still. *Play with my toys.*
She's in the next room doing grown up things, causing
the walls to foam at the mouth. I heard the laughter
of the mattress, I know now all giggles aren't innocent.
Momma's sweat tickling the foot of the bed, I need
to know why her door is always closed, why this *door*
is always closed.

    2.   Some doors are meant to be kept shut

Most open freely. Yet, hers stubborn-eyed stares me
down. I tumbleweed, black ops crawl across living room,
waiting for her to walk out and hold me.
(She never does) Yells from the other side, *it's all alright.*

The lights are off cause most days she can't bear
the ugly in her reflection, how I can't bear the beauty
in her lies.

Sparks fly, gun smoke rises from the locks like there's
fire buried in the cartilage of her bedroom. I know
flames mean sex. I tell myself there are bodies burning
in there. To this day I can't forget the smell of charred
flesh.

3. Fumbling with keys might kill someone

I just wanted to play superhero, and save her. Fears
noosed around neck, caped. Can't fly through
the windows, so I have to break down the door, pick
the locks, fling it open. "Mommy I'm here to save you!"
But, she doesn't need saving—no repentance.

4. Be sure your prepared for what's awaiting on the
    other side

I see her lying on a stack of bones that don't belong
to my father. Broken wedding vows scattered across
the floor.

Keep these *doors* closed, because I hate reliving
what's behind them. I've been sitting on the edge
of my eyes asking my vision the meaning of regret.

5. Once open, you can't unlearn what you've seen

Fornication is the reason I cheat on tests. Reason my
chest doesn't hold my pulse how I'd like it to. I hold
the beating in the gutted of my palm. I've only slammed
the door on my heart once, when I was nine.

I'm 18, tired of talking to notebooks, to doors.
She needs to open up to me.

... Turn the music down, 'cause
 I can't stand the creaking of hinges.

Shattering Water

It rained the night I broke a heart.
The poet in me looked for symbolism in this.
I found none lurking in this maze of liquid, but
I knew....

Truth begins when ankle and mind argue
about train tracks, intersections and refills
of Zoloft. Bourbon loosening the jaw till it
is levee and dull brass overflowing. Moment
tongue isn't a thorn to someone offering
salvation. It is anvil unlearning gravity,
the burdens held within becoming honest.

I shunned my blood that night.
Weighty things flailing from the mouth—ton
of dumbbells wrestling glass.

I heard cracking.
But ignored, kept throwing
kept pushing, till even my breath
lingered in shards.

"You aint my mother."
Numbed the air, a cursing anesthesia.

She broke, my words hit home,
hit womb. She ran inside, guilt is demon
playing eardrum. They chased her back years,
almost back to addiction: became reason for
rehab.

All because I have yet to master
the art of *"let go, of forgiveness."*
The past cannot be recreated, it is definite.

Staring at each drop, I watched
them paint her face, swirling weary
and crystal.

It rained the night I broke a heart.
This means water too shatters.

Monsoon Season

Rain is viewed as blessing. The pouring of undefiled
water upon the heads of a forsaken people is sign
of something greater. Something beyond the skull not
confined to blood or breath, left to linger outside
the thought's constraints. When summer sinks its teeth
in the projects and brownstones, water erupts from
hydrants. The original form of music scribed on Earth's
staff paper. They dance for it in villages where men
cover themselves in ferns and the hides of animals.
Beckon the sky to break in the name of survival,
in the name of growth. *Shed a tear for us oh Tlaloc, that
we may know of ye graciousness. Deliver your parched
people.* Rain is viewed as plague. The bucketing of
wretched water upon the heads of a merciless people
is sign of punishment—consequence for actions that
cannot be pardoned. The word homicide is derived
from flood—interrogate the fish bones found
in the teeth of mountains. In lands of scatting horizons,
palms are left clinging to eaves as mouths take furlough
from Mardi Gras, and become flares for the choppers.
Pleading for the sky to mend its wounds in the name
of mercy, in the name of forgiveness, *We know not
what we do. Have pity on us.* Whoever controls water,
governs the outcry.

Speaking to Flames
for GG, at my first funeral

J: I thought you'd be a lot bigger!

D: Don't mock me. This figure isn't easy to maintain. Cancerous palates keep this full body grimace in gruesome shape. I flex spades.

J: I meant no disrespect, it's just I envisioned you to be broad shoulder galore. To conquer is to drain faith from praying hands. In ancient Rome the gladiators were muscular, Goliath sized men and you're no slingshot.

D: Requires skill, one only I possess. The reaper has no apprentice. To lack morale, to be un-phased by the beauty of life takes one moored to a glacier. I charm the 3rd shot of whiskey down a throat with no designated driver. This requires an unsanitary disgust I wish upon no man. I am a bloodhound sniffing veins that have long since run dry.

J: Do you have any regrets?

D: No one is deserving.

J: Why her?

D: For all of us there will come a time when the eyes summersault to the back of skull like a possessed slot machine. You hit the jackpot if you've spent your lifetime doing good deeds.

J: So you think she's rich?

D: Believe me, she's up to her chin in gold.

Missing Page: THE KIDS

Son is peeled scabs, disinterest in all things athletic, reptile kisser, collector of weird. Is lonely, bully bull's eye, afraid of the school bell, parking lot and mouthfuls of gravel. Face in spaghetti, lockers contents, Snickers flesh wound, camel, broken back, a sweating palm. Finally rouge gunslinger.

Daughter is unappreciated talent at beauty pageant, mother's lipstick, sex because the other girls have it, back seat lover, hatred for the mirror, liposuction, a brittle haunch at the disco, stomach being pumped. Is "I'm sorry."

Kids are the reason Dick and Jane hire babysitter at Father's next country club banquet, wouldn't want stench of their dirty laundry making everyone else uncomfortable.

Bloodlines Lament
for Daniel and Maurice

I walk Harlem streets, envying
the ghost us. The past we have
deadened. Watch as their memories
bathe in all we have forgotten. Playfully
unaware of the wreckage steadily
impending. I want to hand them
hammers and train the boys we once
were in carpentry-preparation for
the shaking.

Con Artist AKA

Don't hate the playa hate the game

Trickster of many suits
pick pocket the lyric from Sinatra's throat
gold toothed molasses whisperer
one with the shiny cuff links
baby, baby slow down beautiful
I just want to talk to yah
hustler of hearts
I don't bite
you need a man like me, one who'd be good to you
slow creep out of bed before night heals
reservations with an empty chair
what you say we get out of here, go back to my place
slaughterhouse with no alarm system
I'm different from all those other guys, trust me
I can change
8 summers verbatim
you believe me right?
Bouquet of thorns
quit playing girl, you know I love you

Dog Breeders

*Wedding rings are expensive leashes. Man,
should not allow self to be chained to steel
breastplate of any woman*—mantra the streets
bicep hums.

Masculine half of the genome has taught heart
to sprout teeth: Cannibalism 101. To be
accepted in this clan of paws one must drool
in the presence of thighs and howl at any
crescent shaped ass dilating the pupil.

If his eyes are anchored in the proper way
to view a woman, he is shunned. Most are sons
of illegitimacy, comfortable being the wood
for chivalry's coffin.

Snarling realization—I am beast because of my
surroundings. Told, *don't remember the names
of girlfriends so as not to make a mistake.*

Tug of war, battle between: gentleman and slip
out when moon moguls the sky.
Who wins if the rope snaps?

It's either canine will love singular or plural.
Savage held dormant by a desire to be more
than my blood. Beast frothing at the mouth has
learned to muzzle his d**k.

Fear not if I'm seen parading the streets with no
leash or collar. Tamed is the one who can roar
but decides to bark.

The Mechanic

*It takes one god, or a singular burst of energy to screw
breath into a lung.*
This he understands. Knows the ocean envies the pool
for its plagiarism. Has come to accept the body
as the last syllable of bad news. Questions if walls
define a room, if so place him in a room of skin unlike
the body and wait for nothing to come knocking.

An addict of repair, reflection of all things broken he is.
Brethren to oil, grease ball, beer bellied men, legacy
of metallic stereotype balding at the crown. Distance
measured in dial tones, *what is time to the ageless eye?*
On duty 24/7, the exploitation of light. Knees have
invested sand in the salt-worn mouths of deities. If he
cannot, *stop believing*, all is lost.

His hands are: shore for the ship wrecked, scripture for
the downtrodden. *How does one fix an illusion?* He
stubs his toe on what's not there. *Looking for flaws
is a lonely profession.* Some nights he brings the job
home with him—a bag of things left to mend:
carburetor, boiler and marriages—an arrangement of
simple complexities, the paradox of living.

*How can one whose footprints are a monkey wrenches
template be broken?* Sees the apartness in all, yet he
cannot correct himself. His history is jigsaw puzzle.
*Costumers dwindle when shop is set up in a garage
of shortcomings.* His toolbox is a back stabbing
confidant. He is learning *love is the strongest tool.*

STEP 4

MONUMENT AMONGST RUBBLE

You Became Ice Sickles

Not much poem in this poem
Just the story of two boys,
Forces of nature, test of will
And hamstring

Blizzard has a long rap sheet
For hit 'n run on city intersections
Collision of white against all that's hard
In New York
(Pavement, bodega's awning, slurs)

It's Sunday night
Buses, taxi cabs, pride
Litter the streets
My brother Sean and I
Commuting from Harlem—
(Gentrified cemetery that 125th is)
To the cliff edge of the Bronx
(Co-Op City, white man's project)

Our plan: D train to Fordham,
Hail a cab and we're free
Simple
A shrill vacancy, as we emerged from
Buck-toothed mouth of subway

"I think we going to have to walk it brah"

3 point too many miles
"This feels like some day after tomorrow shit"
The apocalypse had waltzed through town

Rumor has it, this type of skin
Isn't fond of frost
But we trekked 4 hours

For the moment our footprints owned
This land, traffic lights gossiping
(You see those dumb boys in all that snow,
Where the hell they mommas)
Had to be insane
Allow ourselves, mummified
In this flux of snow, and morning sniffles

Occasionally cars crept along, caution
Evident in the wheels reluctant rotation
Windshield wipers swaying
But, good Samaritans are hard to come by

Black ice in its eyes
This City's audience to survival

Wind likes to leave no evidence of where it's been
Tire marks covered
No traces of humanity
Just us

Lincoln Town Car Travels

Thumb pressed against New York City concrete is catalyst for junkyard pileup. A fleet of cabs flex their horns vying for your dollar, unless you look (black) suspicious.

Wanting to return home before rain begins its reign in Harlem, I search the faces of drivers believing those with scars above the eye know routes to the Bronx. One resembles butchered meat—I am assured we won't get lost.

Traffic makes room for conversation. He initiates by asking if I'd like to listen to the radio. I reply no, my pulse is enough for tonight. At a stop sign two women practice their witchcraft, lower bodies taunting our necks to twist (they do).

Any girl can let cloth hang above the knees in heat, but winter is where you find a woman. I like one wearing a ¾ length leather coat he tells me. Laughing, I nod my head in approval at the absence of misogyny.

A glance at rearview mirror reveals my lack of hair/razor bumps, so he gauges my age, *You in 11th or 12th grade*, he asks. I tell him *I'm a senior*. His skin releases beams of nostalgia—

What you doing after school? College, congrats man! Are you going to your prom? I was prom king back in 1997. I remember being on the D train the night before begging god to let me win prom king. My friends said I had it in the bag, I was the popular type. (The Hutch becomes a High School hallway) *Those were the best years of my life, only reason I wouldn't go back is because of my boy, he's my world. My mother died when I was three and my aunt raised me…*

The car came to a halt. He said *Have a good night, I appreciate you listening.* I said, *Get home safe.* Thinking "I appreciate you not asking to be paid before we pulled off." *Struggle* is synonymous for "I understand," it

makes sibling out of oil and water. As the car
faded into the intersection, I'm left with regret,
we should've exchanged names.

Ode to Ohio

I once thought: half empty glass of you
Smudge on the bathroom mirror
Stain I can't bleach back to genesis
The linguist stern lecture
Reason for weeping
Sulked in a language, I didn't know
My eyes spoke
To be honest, you're not
Worth mentioning
Besides your steady stint with freight trains
A river that's not completely yours
Ordinary state—hills, potholes
Highways blanketed by road kill
Overzealous citizens who believe you're
The star that shines brightest on this
Country's flag
You're not what we urban folk
Call the "life of the party"
No disco ball whirling through your
Vineyards
Muscadines not dripping from the sky's
Thirsty wrist
You've been helpful
7th most populous
I'm sure you're a total asshole
Chest out, chin pointing north
Slums of a masculine bravado
Wind twirling the redwoods cavalier
I don't expect you to have the slightest
Idea of what you put me through

In the 8th grade, telephone to ear
I listened to the nomadic hum of my
Mother's bus down a foreign route
That led her away from my bones
516 miles between
Me and the first woman I've ever loved
I'm sure it sounds unusual
But, thank you
Your name means hope
Means future blind folded though
It may be
Garden of mornings

Ohio
You taught her how to believe
In power of self
Skydiving with no prayer
To call a parachute
The anatomy of triumph
Convinced there's some mystic
Pollutant humming songs of tomorrow
In the air
I've come to realize that you were
Salvation in a thief's garments
I apologize for the cautious leers
There were precious valuables at stake

The process of healing and repentance
Is not universal, this I have learned
My brother dipped his toes into your springs
Unfortunately, he is immune
To your guidance
No worries, alternate methods
Will be found

Thanks for the light.

Tree Hugger

Three boys realize the vacancy
in tomorrow. Brain's introduction to
lofty consciousness—lungs tarnished
by smoke. Teetering the thin line
between reality and sky. They're
bodies draped in forest so as to elude
siren's wrath. Cipher: lips, syringe to
nature's hazy exhale. Pupils
negotiate with blurry darkness.
Hippies seeking peace of mind.

There is a tree in this sprained neck
of the woods, its roots tangled in
a grim silence. It is target for the
young grass hoppers fist. Bow in
respect for the Sensei air is. Practice
their jujitsu on bark. Knuckles coated
in brass, earth will interpret the jazz
in a punch. Whittling their absence
into bull's-eye, the markings will
testify something existed.

Loathsome lumberjacks, searching for
purpose in the vandalism of the spirit.
Three boys will small talk about
shotgun shells. How many it'll take to
drop a grizzly to its knees in prayer.
(Ruffling leaves lead to twig snapping)
Out of fear three boys will run out
of their souls, trying to escape death.

Tonight, death is a raccoon
rummaging through litter, searching
for food.

0,7,1,9,9,3

Lucky numbers

0- Life originated with breath, vows to be more than a place holder.
7- Symbol of perfection, after six there is a day of rest, Earth will part rhythmically like the phase of applause before   sound.
1- You contain many selves: your presence will be a contradiction, to be one—a compilation of multitudes.
9- You will be mistaken for a six. Claim your identity.
3- An atom consist of three constituents, energy's skeleton you are a sun's fever.
71- She is, last night his grandmother hinted to the fact that she is dying, hairline fracture of an hourglass. He questions how a desert can exhaust its sand.
19- Age eldest brother defines home as prison cell and not music of Harlem, rent free living.
93- Terrorism in New York's first draft, bomb in the parking lot that needs editing, this manuscript needs editing.

07-19-93
Misfortune born, birth
day. His father singed into
nonexistence—mother
begins to believe in
miracles.

>Fortune:
>"You find beauty in
>   ordinary things, do not
>   lose this ability"

Brew

1 Grande Java Chip Frappacino extra shot of espresso
Topped with whipped cream, hold the fudge

Spiraled from the lips of the man in the trench coat,
taping his fingers against the countertop suggesting his
car is double parked outside in the gleaming sun. I looked
on from the back of this chic café, with a cup of steaming
hot coco—I let sit to avoid the tongue's misery—my
laptop and thoughts of doing this *here* for a living. My
future aglow in the knuckles of these lyric soothsayers,
in their stained teeth, ink blots, I imagine their bodies
writing all that I am. I say to myself *I'm here too*, so I begin
typing trying to keep up with who I aspire to be, elevator
music calming, hovers loosely like an untamed strand of
smoke. I got *"flow"* now, writing poems about a boy who
sees his work in newspapers, national journals, pressed
against the ocean. He's sitting at a table, shoulders
squared, works of art gloating all around him, sipping
a hot cup of java (graduated from the small stuff). With
a scorched mouth, thumbing through pages of mistakes,
how he lost himself—when the sharp shatter of a coffee
mug meeting ceramic tiles causes me to lose my train
of thought, I notice the guy in the trench coat, *face sour.*

Excuse me Ma'am, this isn't what I ordered.

Wombs Bloom

Woman's lyric is paralyzing—headlights to deer. A soft
gospel lining the throat: to love monotone with stain
glass inflections, at times irritating—poison ivy vines
wrapped around retinas gouged out blind, yet soothing,
how lilac makes the skin prayer or doves dipping
their wings in chamomile to help the sky sleep.

I hear their songs, each sung on a different chord
due to circumstance. Contraction to ear can be likened
to sunlight dripping into the slightly perched lips
of a rose swelling.

For the single mother, one paycheck split between
three mouths, blue moons bulging in your teeth
attempting to eat the night out of a home. You are
a synonym for strength. Let no man forsake the waters
of his initial baptism. Breastfeed your son's soil, so from
birth they possess the concept of growth. Tuck them
tight under their flowerbeds, whisper into their leaves
You will be more than your fathers.

For the woman, shades and an anchored smile, tell him
no more! (Hammers can dislocate the leg of a man
faster than they can nail the leg of a table.)

For the bastard daughter, remember one missing rib
doesn't make you any less of woman.

For mother, *I forgive you.* You learned to love me in 12
steps but you learned nonetheless.

For the womb, life sprouts in all seasons. Cherish the
hands willing to cultivate and remain
for the blooming—
  there are few.

Carnival

for you, I have learned love comes with many apologies. This is one.

The air between us is festive, marvelous
calligraphy of fire and music defining blood's
boiling point. As we drift back to human,
an aerial ballet, free falls from lips euphoria.
We lie there, love lies there just a simmering.

Conversations about feelings can be likened
to gum on sidewalk. We avoid them, till
mistakenly we step into a vulnerable
nakedness, as you describe bustling fairgrounds
clustered in your bones. Telling me this *feeling*
reminds you of the carnival. Your insides
spinning into a honey comb of cobwebs, soft &
fluff, ready to melt on the tongue of a boy who
is beginning to accept his manhood. The hearth
of your existence reduced to whispers as you
bear all.

Next, explaining your fear of holding things that
are not yours: a heart, hands. You relay one
of your many theories. Utter that you know at
these kinds of festivals many wear costumes,
how you've encountered men, who were fun
house mirrors veiled in flesh, but you want to
believe that this is real that I am real.

Silence says much, listening to the unfettered
words lingering on the apex of this moment.
I interrupt your steady ballad with a question—
Can you measure this love on a scale of heart to
mind?—Breath blushes insecure, babbling in
circles. Describe it in carnival terms, revealing
for you this is, hammer in hands striking swift
and forceful.

As the sound in the room fades, the quiet
throbbing, pleading for my response.

I too have the fairgrounds in me. I understand
that they'll be ups and downs, but we are bolts
in a coaster's harness.

These arms are large for many reasons.
Hammer in hand striking swift and forceful,
the ball rises splitting the bell in two and it
dings, it's still dinging, an echo trapped within
this vessel of bone.

I only ask that you make this here, sandwiched
between our bodies be more than temporary.
The carnival doesn't stay for long, it stops,
unloads for a few holy sunsets and keeps
moving, to another town, a new pair
of deserving hearts. Those left behind are
steady chasing what has already escaped them.

So tonight as darkness monopolizes the sky,
we'll put our criminal disguises on: you dress up
as a girl with two pulses, I'll be world's
strongest man. Scale the barbwire fences
of ourselves, break into these *feelings*
and punch holes into their tires. So when they
try to pack up and roll out to a new set
of bodies, they're stuck in ours
a little while longer.

11E

Home is womb, meaning rebirth. This thicket of brick, sky under its rustic nails has been haven for three hearts. The ceiling fan no longer sings the blues, it spins blissful lyric. Upon moving we decided our boxes had no room for misery and bad blood. This is a place of light, we leave our shadows at the front door. The family comes and gathers on special occasions. It becomes a barrack for troops of young ones, who march up and down the foyer screaming their joys. Grandma and Bert are older now. The boulders they once were are gradually phasing to sand. So we cherish every moment in each other's company. Grandma no longer dances at the crack of dawn, yet she knows where to find me if her two-step ever needs a twin. Bert is still in his chair, nonchalant as ever. Today they are palms pushing me toward college. I have never witnessed such pride than them at my graduation. Their veins pumped neon. They sat in that auditorium glowing like the fullest moon. In an instant I was no longer a blueprint but the structure they had hands in building. This apartment cradles rock. It is architecture's birthplace. Sheltered by these walls, I learned that in order to become *self* sometimes takes unexpected wrecking ball. We built this *home*.

Sometimes all it takes is FAITH

There's a woman 3 decades
Away from me, at the other end of the train
Preaching her skin
Holy Ghost numbing her breath
Walks with an impending fever in stride
Graceful down the cart

Now 2 decades
Adjacent to a drunkard, body sprawled
Along the hard seats
The opening doors steal my attention
For a moment
I'm back at her, transfigured
Cloaked in a winter's white wedding dress
Palms gripping the stems of wilted roses
Face a canvas for mascara watercolor
I see a bride to be left, waiting at the alter—
Her groom missing
(Slouches in his barstool, orders one more round)

Now younger than me
A man with irises dyed in thorns
Throws a wink at a daughter
A hard stare strips her matchstick
Naked

Woman pigtails and Sunday dress
Twirling a cracked smile
Just 4 years old
Trying to convert the train
Hands cupped, around her father's finger prints
Peeled them the night before from inner thighs

Today, she stands within inches of me
*"Son look around, you don't have to
end up like them"*
(Offers me Jesus's business cards)
"Look at what he's done for me"

WARRANTY

HEART IS THE ONLY TOOL YOU NEED

Philomath Says No to a Book

The greatest of thinkers are the least social.
Logic with no tongue for manifestation. Einstein
adopted children because he was unable to
calculate the formula for love making. His wife's
nakedness—profession rather pleasure.
A conundrum this orator of numbers could not
solve. Rumor has it, that when discussing
astrological findings Sir Isaac Newton wept
in a spectrum of colors. He realized each star
had a mate to become constellation. But, there
is no mistress for scholars of proportion. Foolish
is the one waiting for a chariot in fields
of contemplation. He who attempts to uncover
the physics of a kiss is dust to a bookshelf.
There is lesson in the embrace that gets knee to
question gravity's birthright. Philosophy trickles
down bloodlines. Yet, love is not inherited.
It is not a gesture for understanding, unless one
understands the heart: its aches and mirth, how
it shatters, refracting (light)-symbol of thought.
However, it is not conceived, one cannot study
love—theoretical state of being, citizen
of imagination. Even when the brain is sleep
thoughts wander, too is true of love, in hate it
persists. Emotion is more than the static
of nerve endings. It is this body assuring
another that it is here for the long run, it is a
chest whispering *I won't desert you*. How genius
can one be, if they fail to realize that the mind
too turns to ash. Death allows no carry on. Yet,
there is movement in the stillest of states.
When the limbs stop responding the heart
continues beating some moments after. This is
not theory but law that love lives on.

Metronome

Skin thinks therapeutic the splinter—
after soaking in a lake of reeds. Sax's
interlude puppets mind to a limb
and you sway subtle as Golden Gate.
Davis, though brass dented didn't stop
catering plates of jazz. Though flesh be
cut, bleeding humanly maroon,
it heals, the arms relearn the gift of
holding, solider to his harmonica. No
voice can mend the jagged hyphen
jutting through vinyl. But, history is
a record causing bodies to swing, doo-
wop tempting lips to find another. If
one has song one is never lonely.
Hands will find camaraderie within
the fingers of a piano. Let chin never
rest on cement. The eye almond
shelled, focused on beyond. This life is
music, long after the note is played or
breath escapes mouth, the only proof
of its existence is in echo that survives.

Growing Down

Pendulums can't fathom
The amputated hands of grandfather clocks
They only swing, rocking forth back clumsy—
Dancing hammock with two left feet
Sober rocking chairs in graveyards
Full of yesterdays, the skeletons of aborted
Childhoods, mummified heartbeats
And honeysuckle

This one is for you:
Freckle faced girl with pig tails
Boy school yard fist and a craving for paste

Once timid, budding oleanders trying
To blossom under an opaque summer's gaze
Bouquets of gust wrapped in the fabric of sail like
Horizons: broken compass, needle in vain
We got false sense of direction
A ship wrecked sunrise off the coast
Of our futures

I skipped a prayer across the undertow, begging
God to bring our early days back to shore

July, yet the June bugs are spider
Webbed stuck in the past as we ought to be
Remember we Fred Astaire across timelines?
No century out of bounds, leap frog
The Renaissance, played kick-the-can with knights
At the Roundtable
Excalibur couldn't joust the streetlights, night
Dawned on us like prophesy
Time machines bring us home,
Before the lanterns start howling, before
Mother is belts, switches and slippers

You! Bonfire of laughter ignited
In the woods of a classroom, have you
Unlearned the scent of finger painted
Hurricanes?
Skies throw temper tantrums too
Our palms weary, full of mourning lighting bugs
Caught in the clenched teeth of cookie jars

What can I steal from tomorrow?

Body's breathing—hula hooping smokestacks
Boys polished in silk seamless, frolicking
Floorboards and mascara
The applause of red stilettos, marching
Chalk outline
His mother *take those off, boys don't do stuff*
Like that

None of it mattered
Rainbows were just rainbows
We were young, premature
Revolutions and incubators
We knew nothing of sparrows and buzzing
Stingers

But, somewhere along the commute
From mud stained trousers to neck ties
We forgot our fathers were fire trucks
And a siren's cyclone
What are colors?
Who cares, my best friend's skin is
Choked mahogany or pale shades of nothing
Settled for the cooperate, maple wood
Desks and paper weights
We dreamt of celestial, juggling moon dust
Orion vibrant
Kid's jungle vine swaying through cabbage patches
Love never fist fights and signatures
Just *"check yes if you do, no if you don't,*
Maybe if your lungs are still unsure"

You
Probably think I'm three wrinkled
Decades to young to understand
The stretch of growing up
I'm young, but I know
I don't want to be gutted ledger,
Gargling history, attempting to
Teach the rocking chair of me
Its childhood

Advice for when you have had enough

You don't have to be so nocturnal
Come out, the "light" is fine.

The Mechanic

This is me, unfamiliar to even my eyes. It has been many moons since I've seen myself whole. It cannot be considered a story if the character does not wield his own tongue. I spent what felt like ions stranded in a jungle of wrenches and jackhammers that jutted from the depths of me. I found myself lost in this body.

I do not know where the blood stream changed courses, but never had I felt so alone with myself.

If you allow people to call you The Mechanic, you have permission to be broken. It is an escape route, retreating out some abandoned tunnel unknown to foreigners of this body. Its downside—as The Mechanic you are expected to fix. How can I mend with the same hands that have torn?

You begin spending nights surrounding yourself with mirrors, people that will share opinions only if you stare hard enough. You learn to love soft, kiss with lips laced in feathers because you cannot be responsible for another tragedy.

I realized this was sin and my knees were already bruised.

The Mechanic is a junkie searching for a fix, but, now I am comfortable in this shattered, in this junkyard being lowered into wishing well. No longer will I pretend to not need rain during drought. The Mechanic is only a title, I am flesh mimicking steel, tool.

Storks Carry Toolboxes

Many, many flocks of them
They have come by the thousand
Parades of feathers flirting
With a skylines benevolence
Silence reeled in the air, lifts their wings
Darting through hostile space
Reflection of throwing knives

Us, in our naturalist of states
Gathered within beaks
Skin honest testimony
To an aged rumor, a flailing myth
On how we got *here*
Subtle question laced in every
Nook and canary dirge
Of our movement
Children of flight, steel, architecture

Our bodies jelly jars of nuts and bolts
Sauntering blueprints
Designed by our own hands

Dust, compass needle crocheted
Into our beings

We are man

Pencil eraser repentance
Cracked but clean slate

Regret is a leash moored to yesterday
Earth may jitterbug shake
Beneath you, your insides
Spilling into a flux of sallow metal,
Burnt brick

There will be days you feel less human
More construction site
Hard hat zone of our psyche
Reduced to caution tape
Victims of the bulldozers haymaker

Yet, your knees
Know nothing of Surrender
We were born toolboxes
Mechanics for life's natural
Malfunctions

We all fall short
Even the church girl,
Mirrors mistress, mascara
And blush improvs
Writer who sweats in cursive
Felon who can't shake the past
Off his orange jumpsuit

Hammers of fate
Body-sized nails holding the sky in place
Second chances will slither
Through marrow
Welcome them with open hearts

Remembering
As long as there's breath
There's time for rebuilding.

A Few Thoughts of Gratitude

This by far is the biggest and most important project I've worked on to date. The amount of dedication it took far exceeded my expectations. There were nights I questioned myself about my own story, whether or not I was willing to welcome the world inside the beautiful wreckage of me. Manual is a reflection of the process and journey I've gone through to get me to this point It is hard to narrow down the people that have helped and guided me with the development of this book, because everyone I've ever encountered has played a role in the development of me as a person. So I sincerely apologize if I neglect to mention some names, trust me when I say I appreciate the moments we've shared and I couldn't have done this without you.

Grandma & Bert
for giving this wandering boy a home to learn to love
Ma
for the struggle and the fight against it
Daniel
for reminding me it's ok to dream
Dad
for being there when you didn't have to
2010 Team
for the greatest year of my life
Joss
for being my 1st and number 1 fan
Kedene
for keeping my head from swelling
Michael Cirelli
for the support and words of wisdom in the right moments
Mahogany Browne (Momma Mo)
for teaching me that the winner is the one who leaves it all on stage
Urban Word NYC
for introducing me to my voice
You
for the time you've shared getting to know me